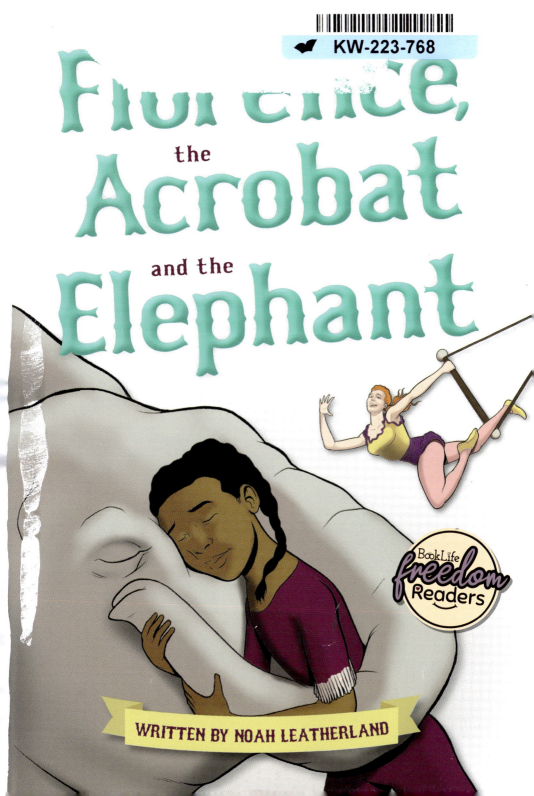

Florence, the Acrobat and the Elephant

BookLife
freedom
Readers

WRITTEN BY NOAH LEATHERLAND

©2024 BOOKLIFE PUBLISHING LTD.
KING'S LYNN, NORFOLK, PE30 4LS, UK

ISBN 978-1-80505-172-5

FSC
www.fsc.org
MIX
Paper | Supporting
responsible forestry
FSC® C195953

FLORENCE, THE ACROBAT AND THE ELEPHANT

WRITTEN BY NOAH LEATHERLAND
BASED ON A STORY BY REBECCA PHILLIPS-BARTLETT
EDITED BY REBECCA PHILLIPS-BARTLETT
ILLUSTRATED BY MARK DINSDALE

ABOUT THE AUTHORS AND ILLUSTRATOR

NOAH IS A LIFELONG FAN OF COMIC BOOKS, VIDEO GAMES, MOVIES AND PRO WRESTLING. TRYING TO TAP INTO ALL THE THINGS THAT MAKE THESE HOBBIES COOL IS WHAT DRIVES NOAH'S WRITING. NOAH WAS A RELUCTANT READER AS A KID (AND STILL IS), SO HE HOPES TO PUT A BIT MORE FUN AND EXCITEMENT INTO CHILDREN'S BOOKS.

REBECCA LOVES STORYTELLING. WHEN SHE IS NOT AT WORK WRITING STORIES, SHE CAN OFTEN BE FOUND AT THE THEATRE TEACHING, PERFORMING OR DIRECTING. REBECCA LIVES WITH HER THREE CATS WHO LOVE TO HELP HER WRITE BY WALKING ACROSS THE KEYBOARD AS SHE IS TYPING.

MARK DINSDALE GOT HIS START IN ILLUSTRATION DRAWING DINOSAURS AND SUPERHEROES IN THE BACK OF MATHS BOOKS WHEN HE SHOULD'VE BEEN LEARNING HIS TIMES TABLES AND HAS BEEN A PROFESSIONAL SINCE 2017 AS LEAD ILLUSTRATOR FOR TWO TOP-NOTCH COMPANIES. WHEN NOT CREATING CAPTIVATING ART, YOU'LL FIND HIM SURROUNDED BY THREE SMELLY BUT ADORABLE CATS AND A WAGGY-TAILED DOG, AND SHARING LIFE'S CANVAS WITH A LOVELY GIRLFRIEND. DON'T BE FOOLED BY HIS WEIRDLY LARGE FOREHEAD – HIS DRAWINGS OCCASIONALLY MAKE PEOPLE GO, "THAT'S NICE" AND IT FILLS HIM WITH JOY UNTIL HE REALISES HE'S DRAWN THE FEET A BIT WEIRD.

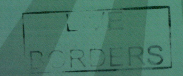

CHAPTER 1

ROLL UP!

Busy factories puffed smoke into London's ever-expanding skyline. The clip-clop of hooves bounced through the streets as horses pulled carts across the city. London was full of hardworking families who had tiring jobs with long hours. So, of course, everyone needed to have some fun after a tough day.

"Roll up! Roll up!"

The loud cries spread through the air as people gathered. In front of the crowd, a man waved them  forward with his cane. Behind him stood a giant circus tent, bright red with white stripes and blue flags draped across it.

"Welcome to The Brilliant Big Top! Come, one and all, to see the most spectacular show on Earth!" the man yelled out. The crowd soon formed a line, chattering to each other as they wondered what The Brilliant Big Top had inside. A hand broke through the tent's curtain.

"You're just in time. Follow me," said a young girl, her voice full of glee as she held the curtain open, welcoming the  people inside. Her name was Florence. Florence had grown up travelling all over the country with

The Brilliant Big Top. As the circus assistant, she made sure all the performers had everything they needed to put on a fantastic show.

Just like every other night, Florence watched as the circus performers dazzled the crowd. The Brilliant Big Top had the most skilled jugglers, clowns, tightrope walkers and acrobats that London had ever seen. But most importantly, it had Gus.

Gus was the most entertaining ringmaster in all of London. Every night, he stood in front of the tent, twirling his cane to draw the audience in. There was no amount of rain, sleet or snow that could stop him from being out there. Braving the elements was worth it because

he knew that his performers put a smile on every face that came to watch.

Florence had seen her friends perform thousands of times before, but she watched them with the same amazement she had the first time she saw them. Florence's favourite part of the show was always her best friend, Elsie the acrobat. Elsie's performance was the most dangerous of all. She swung from the big top's roof on the trapeze swing!

At the end of the show, Gus came backstage with a thunderous applause behind him. "Another fantastic performance, everyone!" Gus cheered. "You were all marvellous!"

"You were amazing, Elsie!" Florence said with a beaming smile.

"Thank you, Flo. I hope you will be up there on the trapeze with me one day," Elsie replied.

As they spoke, a strange figure slipped through the group. Florence watched him, feeling her neck shiver as she followed the mysterious man's creeping footsteps. He was tall and stern like a scarecrow, with a thick moustache and ghostly pale skin. He strode towards Gus and whispered something in the ringmaster's ear. Gus's smile vanished.

"Everyone, I have an announcement to make," Gus said. "Ladies and gentlemen," he began, his voice on the verge of breaking, "this evening was my final performance with you all..."

CHAPTER 2

CHANGES

What was Gus talking about? Florence glanced across the room – everyone was just as stunned as she was.

"I will be handing over my hat to Edgar," Gus said. A disgusting yellow grin grew on the pale man's face as Gus said his name. "I just want to let you all know how much I've enjoyed—"

Edgar's sharp elbow shoved Gus out of the way.

"I can take it from here, thank you,"

Edgar said as he snatched Gus's top hat and cane. "There are going to be some changes around here now that I am in charge. Bring them in, boys!" Edgar snapped his fingers at the two henchmen behind him.

The tent filled with terrible noises as Edgar's men brought in the next big change. Wheels squeaked as heavy metal cages clanked and creaked through the curtain. Florence could not believe her eyes when she spotted what was being kept inside the cages. There  were tigers, seals, monkeys and more beautiful creatures that Florence had only ever seen drawn in books. But these animals did not look the same as the ones in the books. They looked terrified.

"These animals will be taking over your acts," Edgar announced, banging his cane against the rusty bars of the monkey's cage. "You have one week to train them before we reopen the circus."

"One week? How are we supposed to teach these animals our acts?" Elsie asked.

"Did I ask for questions?" Edgar snapped, waving the cane a whisker away from Elsie's face. "Get it done."

Edgar turned on his heel and left, his long black coat flapping behind him. The performers huddled together, looking at each other as their hearts sank to the floor. How could they possibly meet Edgar's ridiculous demands?

Florence scanned across the saddened faces of the performers until her eyes met with one of the animals. She stepped closer to the animal's cage, placing her hand on a cold metal bar. Huddled in the shadows was a young elephant. A dirty bronze plaque was attached to the cage. Florence wiped away the grime with her thumb and felt the letters that were cut into the metal.

"Connie," said Florence, her eyes lifting from the name tag up to the elephant. Florence slowly reached into the cage. Connie's trunk gently landed in Florence's palm. "Hi, Connie. I'm Florence."

CHAPTER 3

LEARNING THE ROPES

In the week that followed, the circus performers did their best to teach the animals how to do their acts. Elsie and the acrobats took on the monkeys. They quickly learnt it is very hard to teach a monkey once they have stolen all the bananas.

The jugglers became seal trainers. Unfortunately, it was quite difficult to teach an animal with flippers to throw and catch. The clowns were left to try to train the tigers. Most of their lessons were spent screaming and running away from the big, dangerous cats.

Nothing was going to plan, except for Florence and Connie. Florence had never been much of a performer, but with Connie, her confidence grew. Florence learnt how to balance on Connie's trunk. Connie learned how to spray water from her trunk hard enough to send Florence flying into the air. As risky as it was, neither of them ever got hurt. They were so gentle with one another and never pushed their tricks too far. The two of them quickly became very good friends. In fact, Florence was making a lot of new friends.

In between training with Connie, Florence took the time to care for all the other animals that had been brought to the circus. Edgar and his men showed no interest in caring for them. So, Florence decided to do it herself. She gave them food and water, scrubbed their cages and played with them. The tigers even let Florence brush their fur when they weren't chasing the clowns.

Soon, Edgar's grand reopening of the big top came around... just as dark clouds were brewing in the sky. As the performers were getting their equipment ready, they heard a deep, booming rumble. Florence peeled back the curtain to look outside. Raindrops stung her face as the wind smacked her cheeks and blew her hair into a mess. Thunderclouds covered the sky like a black sheet.

"The show cannot go on tonight," Elsie said

after pulling Florence back inside and out of the storm. "It's too dangerous to do our acts in this weather."

Edgar sneered at the thought of cancelling the show. "No. The show must go on," he said.

"But..." Elsie tried to argue. However, her protest was cut off by Edgar raising his cane up to her chin.

"The show goes on, or you can all take your things and live on the street!" Edgar yelled. "Now go and get your filthy animals ready!"

CHAPTER 4

THE SHOW MUST GO ON

The rain hammered down onto the big top and the flags barely hung on in the wind. Cracks of lightning flashed in the sky followed by the deep rumblings of thunder. In the middle of it all, Edgar stood in the mud gathering an audience for his first show.

"Roll up! Roll up!" Edgar shouted. Two of Edgar's henchmen held umbrellas over him whilst the audience were left to get soaked in the rain. "Welcome to Edgar's Exotic Extravaganza!"

Florence and Elsie peered out of the tent, watching as the audience lined up to come inside. If only they knew how little Edgar cared about everyone's safety.

"What are we going to do?" Florence looked to Elsie. Surely she would know how to stop Edgar. But Elsie said nothing. What could they do? Edgar was in charge of everything. He clearly did not care that something could go wrong. To him, all that mattered was the fame and fortune. Florence and Elsie quietly watched as the audience entered the tent and found their seats. There was nothing they could do. The show was going on whether they liked it or not.

Florence watched the show from her usual spot by the curtain. She had watched her friends perform hundreds of times before, but with Edgar in charge, this show was very different... and the bad weather was making everything go wrong.

The jugglers tried to do their tricks with the

seals, but strong winds blew through the tent and made them drop everything. The thunder and lightning terrified the tigers. The clowns did their best to calm the tigers down, but every clap of thunder had them hiding away in the corners of their cages. Next up, it was Elsie and the monkeys.

Florence trembled as Elsie and the monkeys climbed up to the trapeze. The rain had started to leak through the big top's roof. The water made the ladders slippery. Each step was more dangerous than the last. Florence's heart rattled against her ribs as she saw Elsie and the monkeys struggle.

"Elsie! You can't do this! It's too dangerous!" Florence shouted. The terrifying wild eyes of the new ringmaster sprang in front of Florence.

"Quiet, girl!" hissed Edgar in Florence's face. "You're lucky I haven't made you pay to watch from here. Just make sure you and that disgusting elephant are ready to go on after this."

Florence's jaw locked shut as Edgar shouted. Her eyes darted back to Elsie, now at the top of the trapeze and getting ready to jump. Elsie had done this stunt more times than she could count. This time, Florence saw Elsie's knees trembling. The rain thudded on the tent above her. The wind shook the platform beneath her feet. The thunder boomed outside. Elsie took one last shaky breath and got ready to jump...

CRASH!

The dreary night was illuminated by a burst of bright orange flames. Florence winced as a choir of screams piped up, the sound matched with the frantic thumps of panicked running. Black smoke puffed through the tent, stinging Florence's eyes.

Florence froze in fright. The ground shook under her, caused by the heavy feet of a charging elephant. Connie ran past her, escaping the burning tent.

"Get that elephant!" Edgar yelled at his men.

"Come on, we need to go!" a familiar voice said. It was Elsie. She grabbed Florence's hand

and led her out of the tent. Mud splashed under the girls' feet as they ran from the burning big top. The kiss of the cold night air finally snapped Florence out of her daze.

She looked around at the chaos. A single lightning bolt was all it took to destroy the only home Florence had ever had.

CHAPTER 5

NOT OUT OF THE WOODS YET

"Connie! Connie!"

Florence tried her best to call out to the elephant, her voice battling the sound of the raging storm.

"Where would she go?" Elsie asked, the mud squelching under their feet as they walked further into the woods. The trees swayed and their branches shook in the wind. The rain soaked the girls as they searched.

Florence and Elsie were not the only ones looking for Connie.

"Bring me back my elephant!" Edgar's voice echoed in the distance. Through the trees, the girls saw Edgar's henchmen, looking for any clues that might lead them to the missing elephant.

Elsie tapped Florence on the shoulder and pointed to something on the ground. Footprints in the mud. Large, round footprints. The girls followed the footprints through the woods and stayed hidden, ducking behind the trees. They could not risk Edgar's henchmen finding Connie first.

Darkness fell around them as the girls went deeper into the woods. Just as they were starting to lose hope, there was a rustle in  the bushes. Florence tiptoed towards the bush and reached out towards it. A long grey trunk reached back out.

"Connie!"

Florence pushed back the branches and there was Connie, huddled over in the cold. Connie wrapped her trunk around Florence and pulled her in close. Florence hugged Connie back, so happy to have found each other once again.

"What are we going to do?" Florence asked Elsie. "We can't make her go back there."

"I guess we will just have to make do and see how long we can stay out here," Elsie replied. With nowhere else to take Connie, the two girls got to work making a camp in the woods. They gathered what they could to make a pair of hammocks. Connie helped hang them from the trees. Then,

they made a soft bed of leaves for Connie to rest on beside them.

The three of them camped in the woods for a few days. It was nice to have some peace and quiet

after Edgar had caused so much trouble at the circus. But they could not stay there forever. They were running out of supplies. It was time to head out of the woods.

CHAPTER 6

THE BREAKOUT

The two girls and the elephant made their way out of the woods. They couldn't really tell which way they were going. When they found Connie, they had been walking through the darkness and the storm. It was easy to get lost.

They wandered through the trees, hoping to find a way out. Elsie pointed ahead of them. The trees were starting to thin out and there was a clearing ahead. Elsie, Florence and Connie crept up to the clearing and there it was: the big top. It was still standing tall,

but it had a large hole from the fire. They must have ended up walking in a circle through the woods. Florence and Elsie panicked, knowing that if Edgar saw them, he would try to take Connie away. Just as they were about to run back into the woods, they saw something.

Something was coming out of the tent. It wasn't Edgar or any of his men. It was a donkey... followed by a hippopotamus... and a giraffe. Edgar must have bought new animals to replace all the ones that had escaped. Surely Edgar wouldn't let them out of their cages?

A hand held the tent curtain open and a seal came bouncing out, dragging itself along the ground with its flippers.

"Go! Get out of here! Quickly!" called the mysterious hero, with a voice Florence and Elsie knew very well.

"Gus!" Florence and Elsie shouted as they ran across the clearing towards him, Connie trampling behind them.

"Elsie! Florence! I'm so sorry, I should have never let Edgar take over the circus," Gus gushed. "I heard about the fire. I had to come and make sure everyone was alright. Then I saw that Edgar had caged up all these poor animals. I just had to do something!"

Florence, Elsie and Gus didn't get to catch up for long.

"Hey! You there!"

Edgar came storming out of the tent, waving

his cane at them.

"You again?" he snarled at Gus. "Stop freeing those animals! They belong to me!"

Gus ran. The animals followed him, desperate to escape Edgar's cages.

"We have to help Gus," said Elsie.

"You two! That's my elephant!" Edgar barked at Elsie and Florence. Just the sight of Edgar was enough to make Connie run away, following Gus and the other animals.

"No!" yelled Edgar. He grabbed two of his men. "Forget about that man. Get my elephant!"

Edgar's men ran after the stampede of escaped animals. Elsie and Florence chased behind. They couldn't let Connie get captured again.

"Oh no!" Elsie shouted as they tried to catch up. "Connie is heading straight into the city!"

CHAPTER 7

PANIC ON THE STREETS OF LONDON

The streets of London were full of life. Shopkeepers called out their prices across the market. Horses galloped down the roads as they pulled carts behind them. Although the streets were packed tight, the busy Londoners could not have possibly known how wild things were about to get.

A donkey burst through the street... then a hippopotamus... a giraffe... a seal... and then an elephant. People dove to the side of the road to get out of the way of the stampeding animals.

The buildings shook as Connie's heavy footsteps thudded along the road. Lots of strange things happen on the streets of London, but the people of the city had never seen anything like this. Just as they got back to their feet, they were shoved out of the way by two of Edgar's men.

"That elephant can't run forever!" one of them shouted as they chased Connie into a park. Just as the other man was about to yell back, something swung over their heads. As it passed over them, it took one of the men's hats and made his bald head shine in the sunlight.

"Yoohoo! Over here!"

Elsie flew through the air above them. She was using a piece of

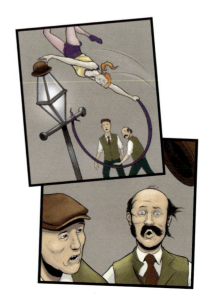

ribbon from the circus to swing off the park's lampposts. She had the man's hat in her hands and placed it on top of the post.

"Hey! Give me my hat back!" the man yelled up at Elsie, the other man laughing at him. Elsie swung away and left the two men to squabble. It took a moment for Edgar's men to remember that they were chasing after Connie.

They looked across the park and all they could see were the trees, a few benches and a grey stone fountain.

"Where has that elephant gone?" one of them asked.

"How can you have lost an elephant?" the other man replied. Edgar's men left the park to look for Connie, arguing as they went.

Florence poked her head out from behind one of the trees. She made sure Edgar's men were out of sight and walked over to the fountain.

"I can't believe we got away with that," Florence said. The fountain stopped spraying water and started to curl up. The water sloshed around and spilled by Florence's feet. Then, a trunk shot water all over Florence.

"Come on! We have to get going!" Florence chuckled as Connie rose out of the fountain's water, coming out of her camouflaged hiding spot.

Florence and Connie went to look for Elsie. As they walked through London, Florence spotted a crowd gathered in Trafalgar Square. Whatever they were watching, they seemed to love it. They cheered and clapped at something that Florence couldn't see. Florence and Connie moved through the crowd and finally caught sight of what had everyone so excited.

It was Elsie! She was swinging from Nelson's Column in the middle of Trafalgar Square, using her ribbon to put on a show for everyone watching. Florence watched Elsie with glee, just like she had in the circus for years. It was the first time she had seen Elsie look so happy since Edgar took the circus from Gus.

Elsie landed perfectly and the crowd burst into a round of applause. The acrobat smiled as she soaked it all in. She looked across and saw Florence and Connie as part of the cheering crowd. As nice as it was to see her friends, it reminded her of the trouble they were in with Edgar.

"You found Connie," Elsie said as she joined her friends again. "Well done, Florence. I guess we had better get back to our camp in the woods."

Florence could tell Elsie wasn't thrilled about the idea. "You miss it, don't you?" Florence said. "I know we can't go back to the circus, but there's no reason that you can't keep performing. It could even help us make some money..."

Elsie looked around at the crowd. Florence was right. There was nothing Elsie loved more than soaring through the air and performing for an audience.

"Let's do it!" Elsie smiled.

CHAPTER 8

THE BEST SHOW IN TOWN

After performing for the crowd in Trafalgar Square, Elsie took her performances all over

London. Elsie drew large crowds in every part of the city. Florence and Connie were

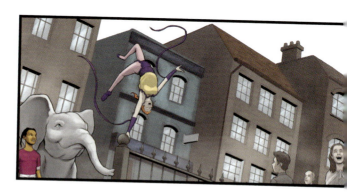

there to support her everywhere she went. Sometimes, Florence and Connie performed in the streets with Elsie. They had never got to

perform with each other in front of a crowd. Edgar's bad decisions had made sure of that.

The three of them made their way around the city and word spread about the amazing acrobats and their elephant. The crowds got bigger and bigger with every performance.

As the crowds got bigger, so did their love for performing. Elsie, Florence and Connie were getting a lot of attention. All that attention had people talking. After their shows, people would come up to Elsie and Florence and tell them how much better they were than the other circus. Could Edgar still be out there?

Elsie and Florence had to find out what had happened to the big top. When Gus was in charge of the circus, there were huge lines of people waiting to get a seat every night. That evening,

there was no one waiting when Elsie and Florence got there.

They wandered up to the curtain and peered inside. The number of people in the crowd could be counted on one hand. Elsie and Florence stayed hidden as the show began. Edgar appeared on the stage, walking on stilts and juggling. He didn't do either very well. Then, he introduced his new animals. Had Edgar captured some of the other animals that ran away? But when the curtain opened, there were no roars or galloping hooves. It was the two men who had chased after Connie... and they were

41

dressed in animal costumes. Florence and Elsie couldn't control their laughter. This was terrible!

Edgar heard their giggles and spotted them.

"YOU!" he boomed, their giggles stopping in an instant. "You did this to me! You stole my elephant! You stole my audience! You ruined my circus!" He pointed at them, his finger trembling in anger. "Get them!"

Edgar's men ran straight for the girls. Elsie and Florence split up as they tried to escape. With nowhere to run, Florence climbed up the ladder to a platform high in the air. At the top, a tightrope stretched across the big top. It was the only place she could avoid being caught. Florence had seen

performers walk across the tightrope plenty of times. How hard could it be?

Florence took the balancing pole and started to walk across the tightrope. It didn't seem too bad… until the rope started to shake. Edgar's men had followed and were walking on the tightrope after her. Florence spun the pole around her, keeping Edgar's men away.

"What are you doing? Catch her already!" shouted Edgar. Edgar ran to the ladder and began climbing up. If his men couldn't catch Florence, he was going to do it himself.

"Florence!" Elsie called out. Florence looked down. Elsie had found someone to help. A grey trunk dipped into the circus pool and took a big gulp. Connie had arrived to save the day. She took aim at Edgar and shot a powerful jet of water at him.

Edgar tumbled off the ladder and fell into the pool with a loud **SPLASH!** The pale man climbed out of the pool, soaking wet and furious.

"That is IT!" he screamed. "I am done with this circus!" He took off the top hat and threw it to the ground. He stomped away in his soggy shoes. His men trudged behind him, looking miserable in their costumes.

"It looks like we've got rid of him," Elsie said as she picked up the top hat.

"What do we do now?" asked Florence. A figure stepped out from behind the curtain. Florence recognised them straight away. "Gus!? What are you doing here?"

"I've been here for every show Edgar has put on, secretly taking care of the animals and freeing them when I could," said Gus. "I couldn't leave, not until I saw what happened to this circus."

"Well, you will just have to make sure it stays open," said Elsie, handing Gus the top hat.

CHAPTER 9

ONE YEAR LATER

A year after Edgar caused all that trouble, things were starting to get back to normal. The Brilliant Big Top was back. Gus had mended the hole that the fire had caused. All the performers had returned, and their amazing acts brought huge crowds back to the big top. Elsie was back on the trapeze, doing what she loved.

Florence never set foot on the tightrope again. She was much happier with her feet

46

firmly on the ground next to Connie. Now, she had a lot more to do backstage. All the other animals that escaped Edgar's cages had been found. Florence gave them a safe place to stay with plenty of room to run around and play. None of the animals would ever have to perform in the circus again.

Unless they wanted to...